ROBOGRAPHICS

SUPER SMART ROBOTS

CLIVE GIFFORD

PowerKiDS press

Published in 2026
by The Rosen Publishing Group, Inc.
2544 Clinton Street, Buffalo, NY 14224

First published in Great Britain in 2022 by Wayland

Artwork: Collaborate Agency
Design: Collaborate Agency
Editor: Nicola Edwards

Cataloging-in-Publication Data
Names: Gifford, Clive.
Title: Super smart robots / Clive Gifford.
Description: Buffalo, NY : PowerKids Press, 2026. | Series: Robographics | Includes glossary and index.
Identifiers: ISBN 9781499454451 (pbk.) | ISBN 9781499454468 (library bound) | ISBN 9781499454475 (ebook)
Subjects: LCSH: Artificial intelligence--Juvenile literature. | Artificial intelligence--Social aspects--Juvenile literature. | Autonomous robots--Juvenile literature.
Classification: LCC Q335.4 G555 2026 | DDC 006.3--dc23

Picture credits:
The publisher would like to thank the following for permission to reproduce their pictures:
AIRBUS: 13
Getty Images: ROB LEVER/AFP via Getty Images 4
Nvidia: 5
Shutterstock: Olga Bugrow 21; catwalker 18; Anton Gvozdikov 27;
Phonlamai Photo 29; Sundry Photography 15
Wikimedia Commons: 19, 26

Manufactured in the United States of America
CPSIA Compliance Information: Batch #CSPK26. For further information contact Rosen Publishing at 1-800-237-9932.

CONTENTS

SUPER SMART SOLUTIONS

Robots already perform very valuable work. Supersmart robots and other devices are being developed to do a whole lot more! Building smarter robots is about equipping machines with the abilities they need to work better by themselves and perform varied and complex tasks.

2,000,000 ...

... the number of hours Brain OS cleaning robots had worked by August 2020, all without human supervision.

Taiwan's IVS (Intelligent Vision System) robot plays chess and can recognize letters to play word games like Scrabble. This research robot learns to identify objects and what it can do with them from their shape, color, size, and location.

BRAINY UPGRADE

Some increasingly smart bots rely on boosts in computing power. NVIDIA's Jetson Xavier NX computer module (above) for future robots is smaller than a credit card but as powerful as a supercomputer!

CLEVER DESIGN

Giving robots more clever sensors and the ability to learn in new ways can also make them smarter. A NAO robot, for instance, can learn a task by mimicking what people do and then storing those actions in its memory.

50+ ...

... the number of sensors packed in a 23-inch (58-cm) NAO robot.

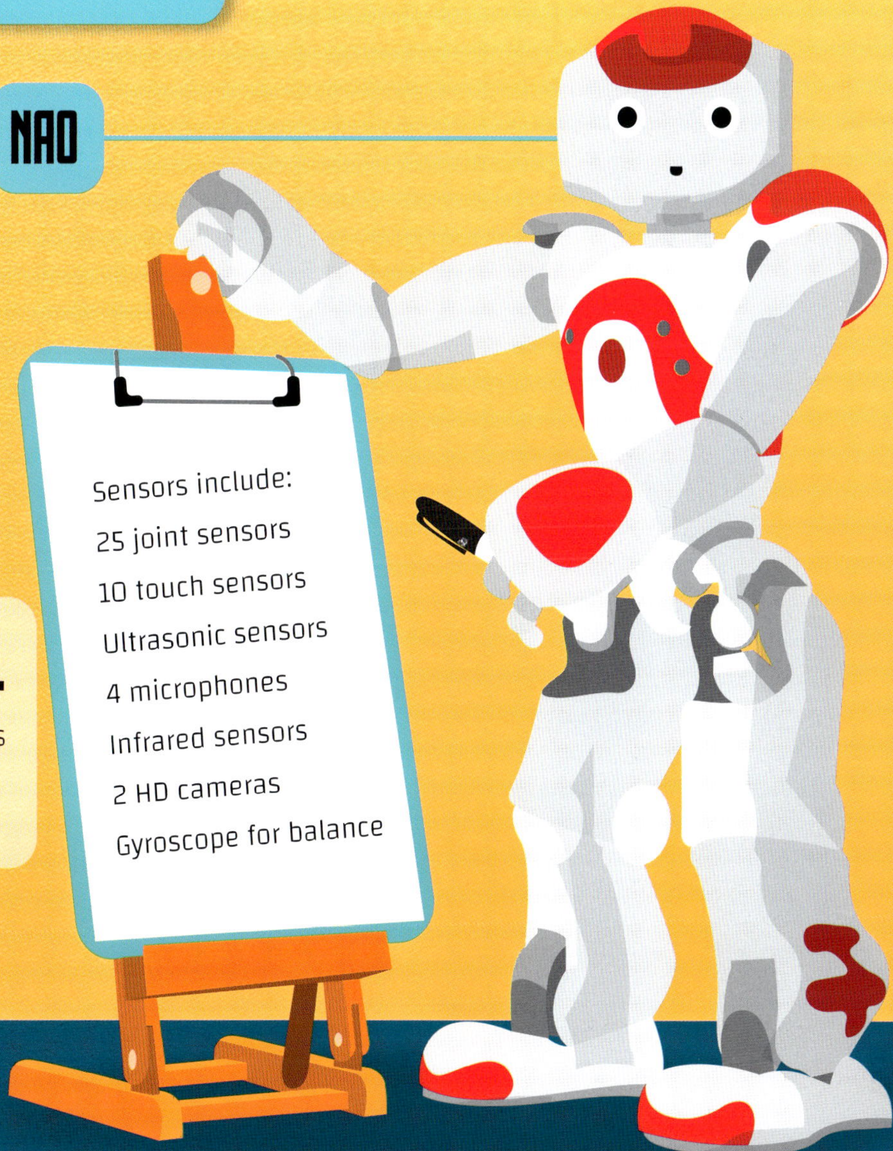

21,000,000,000,000 ...

... the number of calculations this 2.75 x 1.8 inches (70 x 45 mm) computer can make per second.

INDEPENDENT INTELLIGENCE

Early robots relied on costly and slow computers, some the size of an entire room. Once computers soared in performance, shrinking in size and cost, it meant robots could be equipped with powerful computing to run complicated programs.

All the power of a giant 1970s mainframe computer can now be found on a silicon chip the size of your fingernail.

SMART BOT TIMELINE

1921

The word "robot" is first used in Karel Čapek's play *R.U.R: Rossums Universal Robots.*

1961

First robot put to work – the Unimate robot arm, used in car factories.

1973

WABOT-1, the world's first full-sized smart humanoid robot, created in Japan.

1985

A PUMA 560 becomes the first robot to assist in a medical operation.

BETTER THAN US?

Robots can be built to be stronger and able to work for longer than people. They can be more accurate than us, able to repeat the same task to within a fraction of a millimeter time and time again. When these abilities are linked to an intelligent robot's ability to learn, the results can be impressive.

Toyota's sharpshooting CUE3 robot uses sensors in its chest to measure distances. Its joints send feedback signals to its computer controller. This precisely adjusts the angles of the joints so that the robot makes the basketball shot accurately each time.

11.82 ...

... the average number of seconds taken by CUE3 per shot.

1997

IBM Deep Blue computer beats human world chess champion, Garry Kasparov.

2005

Stanley driverless car navigates 175-mile (281-km) off-road course with no human help.

2011

IBM's Watson wins an episode of the U.S. TV quiz show *Jeopardy*.

2019

CUE3 sets record for number of successful basketball shots in a row (2,020 shots).

SOCIAL BOTS

Advances in artificial intelligence and cloud computing are allowing robots to understand speech and access a wealth of information over a computer network. There's a long way to go before a robot becomes your best friend, but some machines are getting sociable.

WHAT DID YOU SAY?

Most social robots can respond to some spoken commands. To understand more complex conversations, some bots send a person's speech to a cloud computing site where the words are analyzed. Keywords and instructions are sent back to the robot to act upon.

21 ...

... the number of different languages the Elias robot foreign language learning app from Finland can recognize. Designed for use with the NAO robot, the program can recognize Korean, Turkish, Japanese, and English words, amongst others.

LIKEABLE LEKA

Not all social robots need to be chatty. Leka plays educational games and interacts with children with learning difficulties using movement, sound, vibration, and lights to grab their attention.

PAWS FOR THOUGHT

Zoetic AI's Kiki robot is a cat devised by robotics expert Mita Yun. As it spends time with its owner, the robot learns and develops its own personality which can be shy, rebellious, loyal, or affectionate. Kiki can be taught new tricks and remember when something she does is liked or disliked.

16 ...

... the number of touch sensors located all over Kiki, allowing owners to pat, tickle, and cuddle the robot.

GETTING EMOTIONAL

Robots don't have real emotions, but some can give responses that appear emotional. For example, a robot might appear sad and regretful if it is told off sharply. The long-term aim is to create robots which people find to be natural and effective companions and colleagues.

100 ...

... the number of facial expressions UBTECH's Alpha Mini robot can create, using large LED screens for eyes.

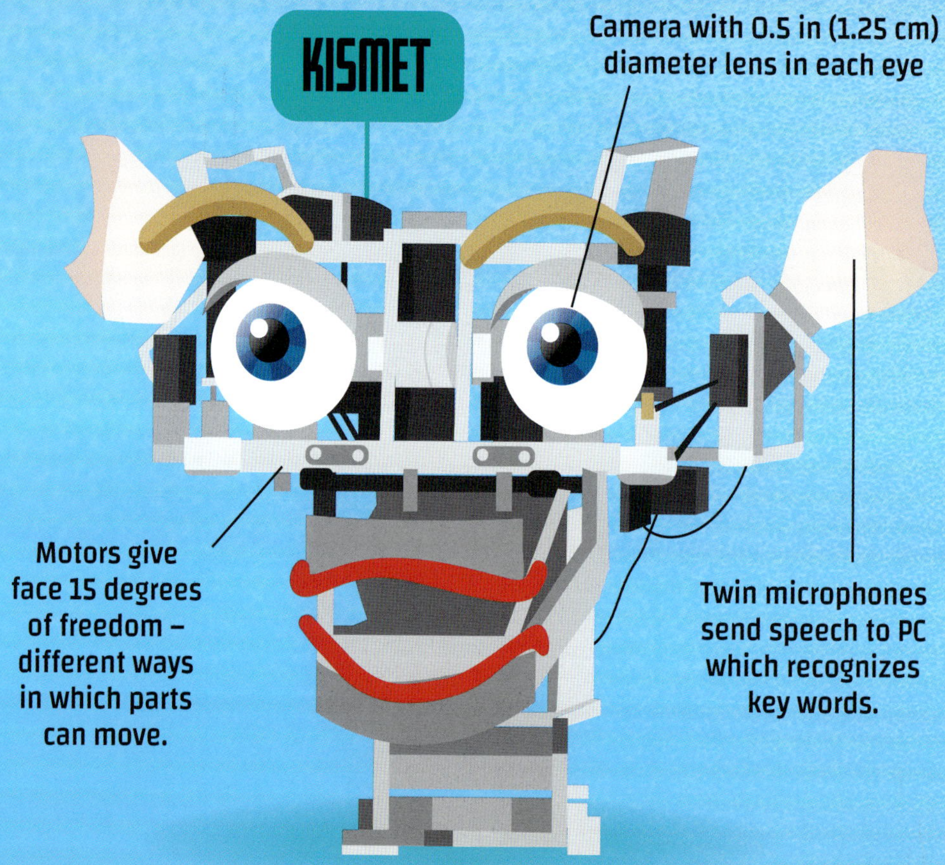

POUTING PIONEER

Built by Cynthia Breazeal in the 1990s, Kismet was one of the first robots to express emotions physically. Multiple motors moved its eyelids, eyebrows, mouth, and ears to form facial expressions. The robot viewed and listened to a person and attempted to respond with a suitable expression.

HAPPY

SURPRISED

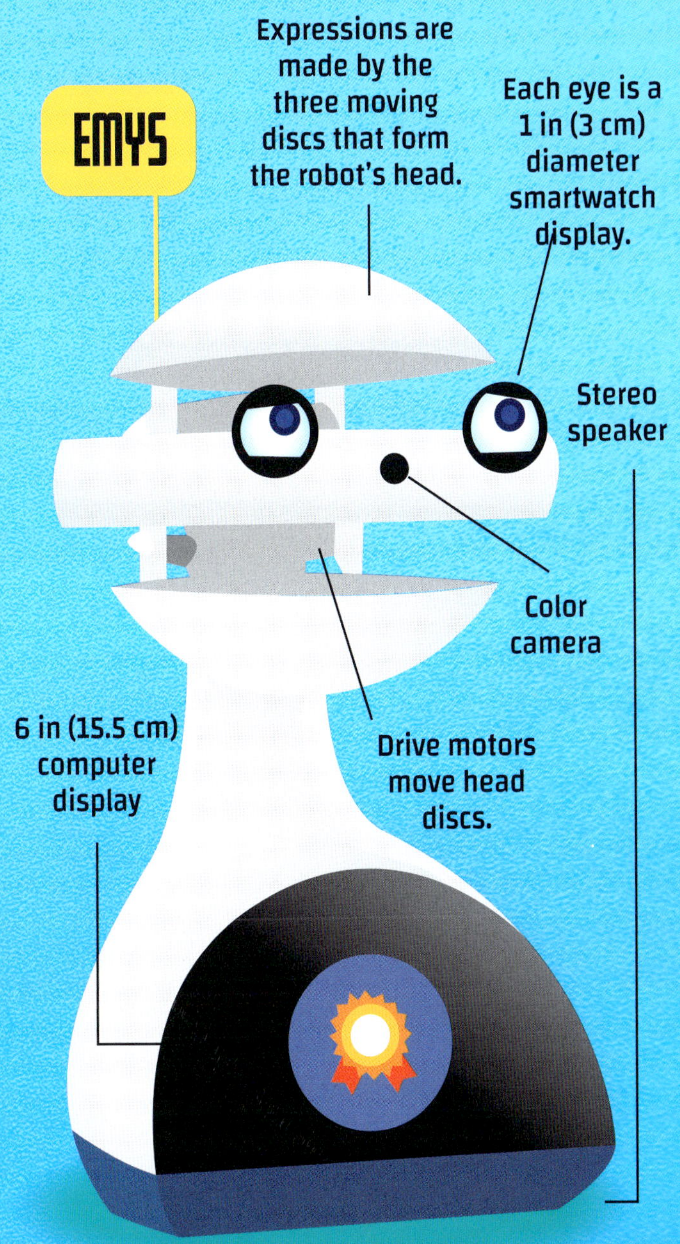

The **Simulative Emotional Expression Robot (SEER)** from Japan uses motion-sensitive cameras. These track human facial expressions as people pass by, which the robot then copies.

MIND YOUR LANGUAGE

Developed in Poland, EMYS is a foreign language teaching robot for young children. The 9 lb (4 kg), 15-inch (37.5 cm) bot expresses emotions including surprise, irritation if its base is pushed, and delight if a child gets a new word right.

4 ...

... the number of touch-sensitive areas on EMYS's head. If stroked, the robot responds by smiling.

SAD

CALM

9 ...

... the number of emotions Kismet could display: happiness, sadness, anger, surprise, tiredness, fear, sternness, disgust, and calm.

PERSONAL ASSISTANTS

Robotic assistants, powered by artificial intelligence, are expected to be one of the most important branches of robotics in the next 20 years. Able to access massive databases, such intelligent assistants could make work easier, faster, and more accurate - and leisure time more fun!

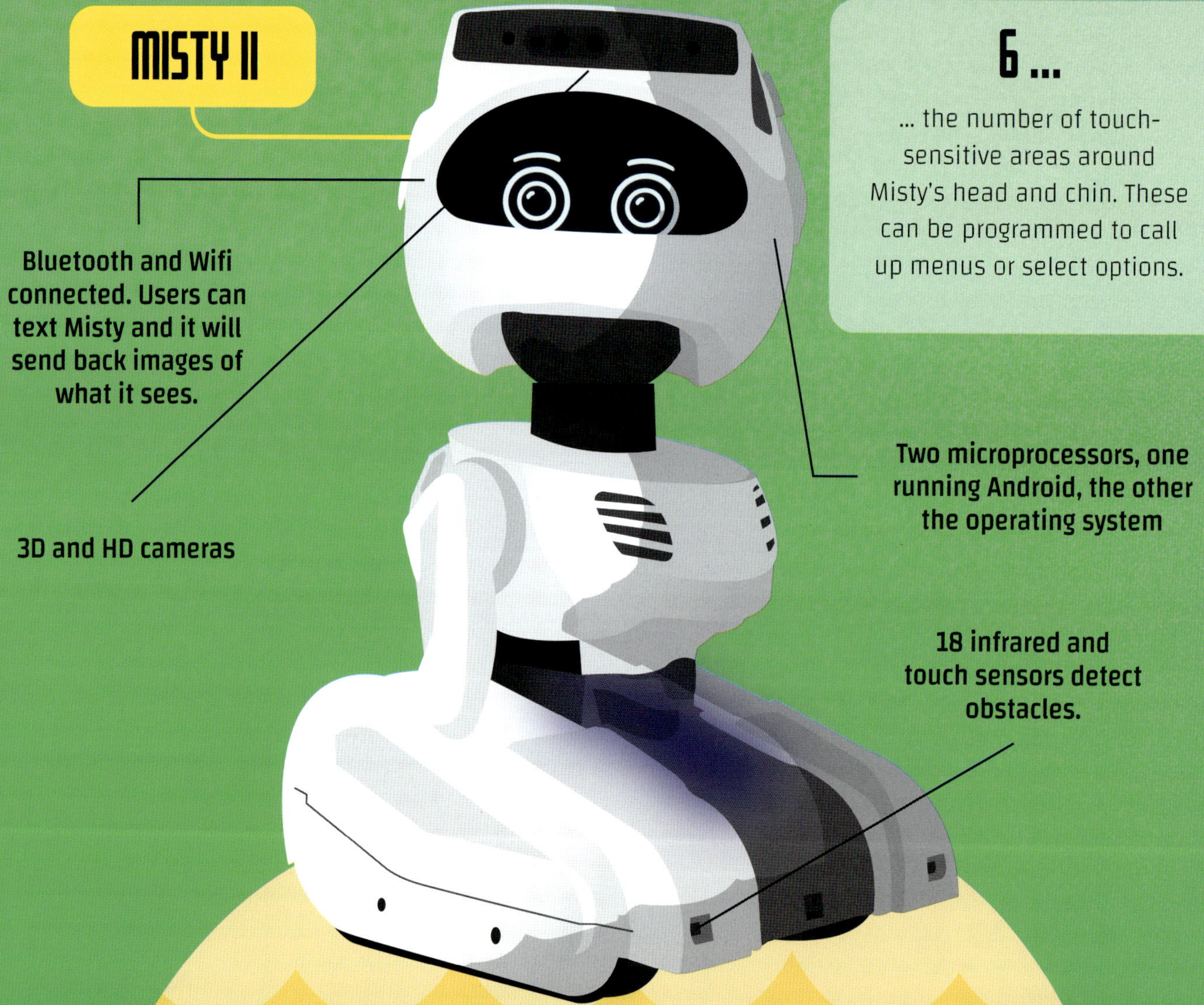

6 ...

... the number of touch-sensitive areas around Misty's head and chin. These can be programmed to call up menus or select options.

MISTY II

This U.S. robot can be programmed to act as a companion, assistant, security guard, or temperature checker in health centers. Misty II can understand voice commands, film and stream HD video, and navigate around a space to fetch and carry small items.

SPACE SIDEKICK

In 2019, a floating astronaut assistant blasted off into space on board a SpaceX Dragon spacecraft. The ball-shaped Cimon-2 from Germany assists astronauts on the International Space Station (ISS) by reading out instructions, answering queries, and giving reminders.

7...

... the number of emotions, CIMON-2 can detect in astronauts' speech: excited, frustrated, polite, rude, sad, sympathetic, and satisfied. The robot can alter its tone of speech in conversation.

Robot's 14 fans move it around and let it shake and nod its head to questions.

Cameras film experiments and are used for facial recognition.

Diameter: 13 in (33 cm)

Weight: 11 lb (5 kg)

Battery life: 3 hours

Mission duration: 3 years

Cameras: 7

Location: 249 miles (400 km) above Earth

Speakers broadcast messages, text instructions, and even play music.

Robot communicates with a cloud computing center on Earth. This processes face and speech recognition data and beams the results back up to the robot instantly.

9 microphones detect sound above the constant 72 Db noise of the ISS (a noise level equal to a vacuum cleaner).

DRIVERLESS VEHICLES

Many AGV (automated guided vehicle) robots travel around factories, hospitals, and offices carrying supplies. Out on the road, though, there's a lot more to contend with. Robotic road vehicles need complex arrays of accurate sensors and powerful controllers to be safe and drive themselves autonomously – without any human supervision.

0-5 ...

... the levels of vehicle automation, with level 5 being completely autonomous. Levels 1 and 2 give a human driver electronic aids, such as parking assistance. Level 4 means the vehicle does all the driving but controls exist for a person to drive if they prefer.

ROBORACE

175 MPH ...

... the top speed of Roborace, the world's fastest autonomous car, achieved in 2019.

1,000,000,000 ...

... the estimated lines of computer code needed to control a single level 5 (completely) autonomous car, according to Jaguar Land Rover.

SAVING LIVES AND THE PLANET

Most road accidents are the result of human error, such as those caused by tiredness or dangerous driving. Driverless cars reduce these threats and their sensors and controller can react quicker to sudden situations, potentially saving thousands of lives. They may also save fuel or electricity by driving in more energy-efficient ways.

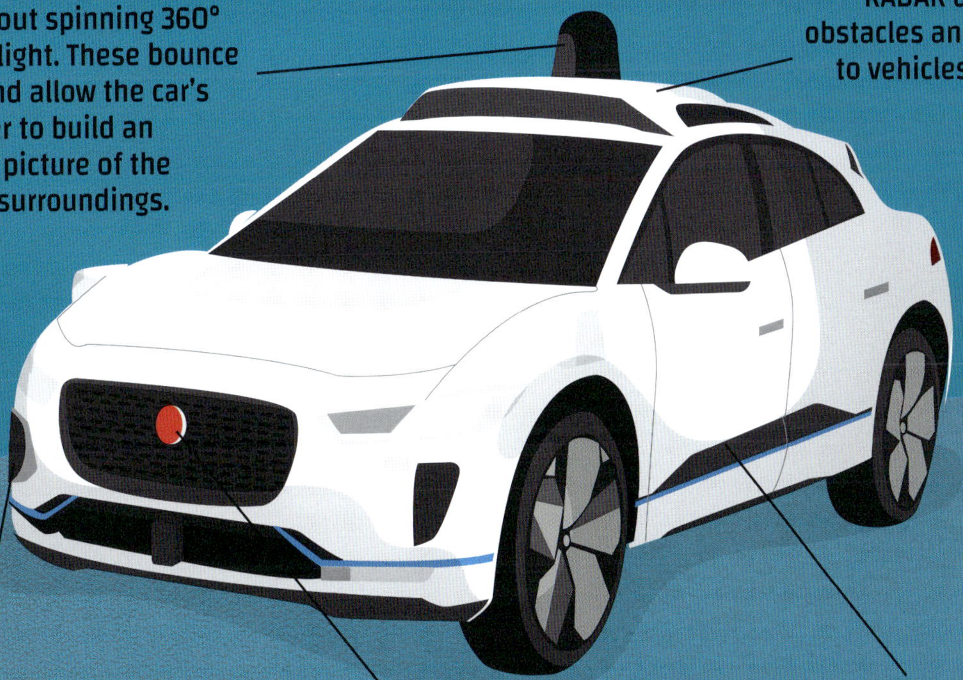

29 ...

... the number of cameras in a Waymo car. These enable the vehicle to spot a stop sign up to 1,640 ft (500 m) away.

20,000,000 ...

... the number of miles driven by Waymo driverless vehicles on US public roads by early 2020.

PROBLEM SOLVERS

To be really useful as machines that work by themselves, robots have to be good at problem-solving. They need to be able to identify what the problem is, and then decide if they can tackle it or if they need to alert human helpers. This all takes machine intelligence.

SPOT THE SOLUTION

Boston Dynamics' Spot robot is a nimble four-legged robot with potential uses in construction, search-and-rescue, healthcare, and other fields. In development, the robot learned how to climb uneven steps, map its surroundings, and open doors.

Length: 3.6 ft (1.1 m)

Total weight: 66 in (30 kg)

Cost: $74,500

DOOR TO DOOR

Many companies are getting excited about using driverless vehicles for deliveries. The problem of how to get the packages from the street to the front door remains. Agility Robotics' Digit may provide an answer. This two-legged robot walker folds up inside the rear of a driverless van, then unfurls itself to carry a package to a door.

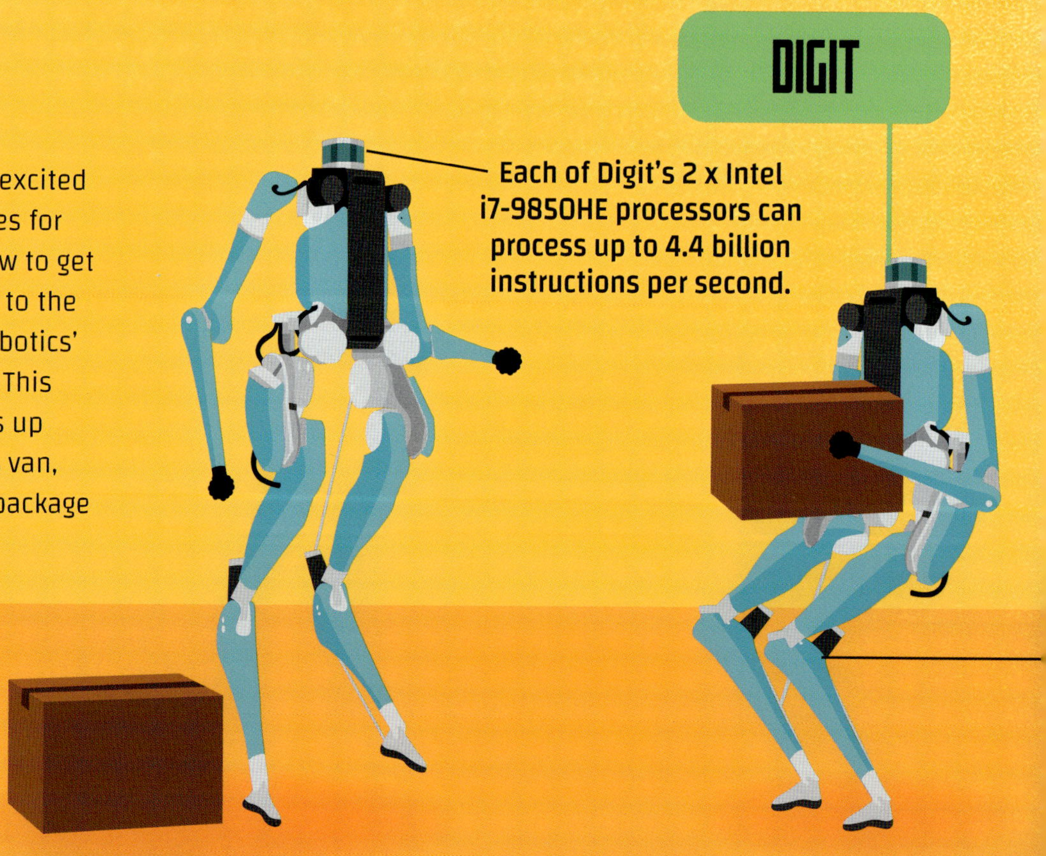

Sensors enable Spot to map 13 ft (4 m) of space around it continually.

SPOT

Keeps its balance, even when walking across uneven surfaces.

5,000 ...

... the number of photos of construction work Spot took each week as it patrolled a 500,500 sq ft (46,500 sq m) building site in Canada.

Can work in temperature range: -4°F to 113°F (-20°C to 45°C)

If its target is barred by a wall or obstacle, Spot looks either side for a way round.

Robot bends at knees to lower package gently. It returns to the van where its batteries can be recharged.

18KG ...

... the maximum parcel weight Digit can carry (42% of its own body weight).

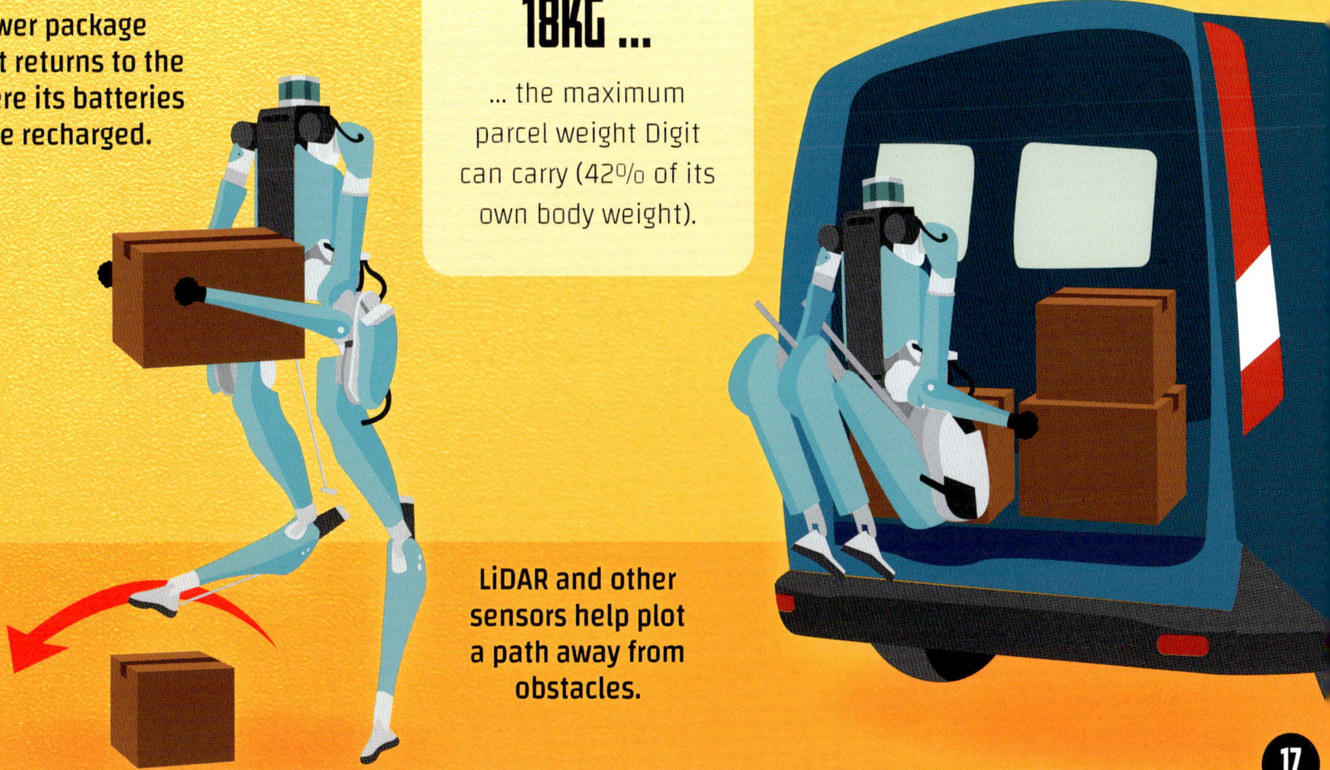

LiDAR and other sensors help plot a path away from obstacles.

ROBOTS LIKE US

Ever since robots were first thought about, people have been fascinated with making machines in their own image. Humanoid robots have to work incredibly hard to match basic human abilities, including balancing, movement, and recognizing and handling objects.

ASIMO

Flexible hands can grip objects, open bottles, and handle tools.

Cameras in head can recognize 10 different human faces.

6 FT (1.3 m)

Asimo can run at a speed of 5.5 mph (9 kph). It would take Asimo 4 hours, 42 minutes to run a marathon.

The robot's twin cameras and controllers can predict a corner and, just like humans, lean the robot into the bend to keep its balance.

STAYING BALANCED

Walking on two legs and climbing steps are abilities we might take for granted, but they're no easy task for robots. They require serious processing power to achieve the same result. Honda's legendary ASIMO robot was the first humanoid to walk up stairs and run with ease, both forward and backward!

Height: 6 ft (1.3 m)

Weight: 119 lb (54 kg)

Walking speed: 1.7 mph (2.7 kph)

NO SWEAT!

Kengoro, built by engineers at the University of Tokyo, mimics the human body more closely than other humanoid robots. Motors pull cables to move Kengoro's fingers and other joints. Parts of the robot heat up during operation, so the robot is cooled by water flowing through tubes. Kengoro appears to sweat as some of the water evaporates through small holes in the robot's aluminum body.

Height:
5.5 ft (1.7 m)

Power consumption:
Up to 140 watts

KENGORO

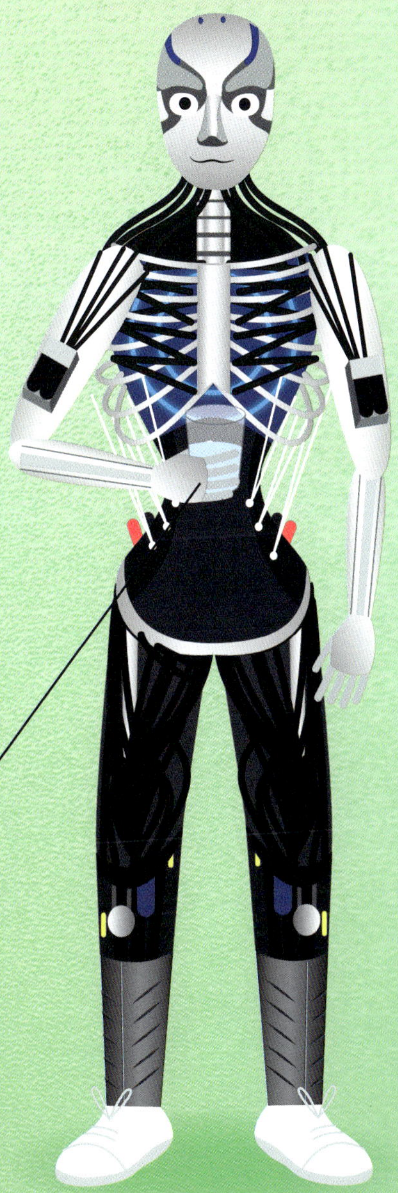

Kengoro needs **half a glass** of deionized (purified) water for cooling each day.

The **15.5-foot (1.7 m)** Surena IV humanoid from Iran has **43 degrees of freedom** enabling it to dance, climb stairs, walk at **0.4 mph (0.7 kph),** and handle all sizes of object, from this large beach ball to small power tools.

Kengoro boasts 174 degrees of freedom, over 110 more than Asimo.

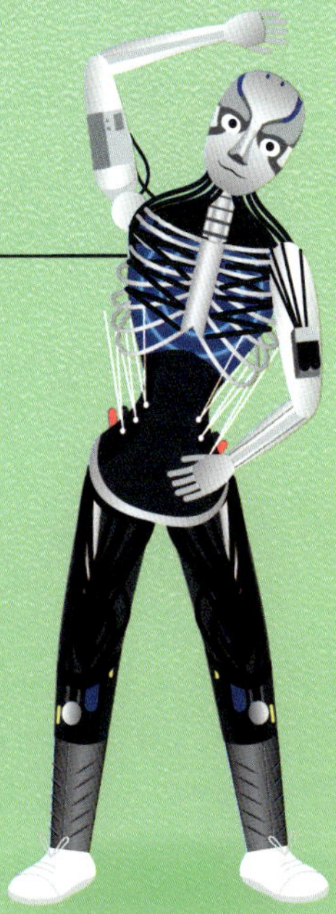

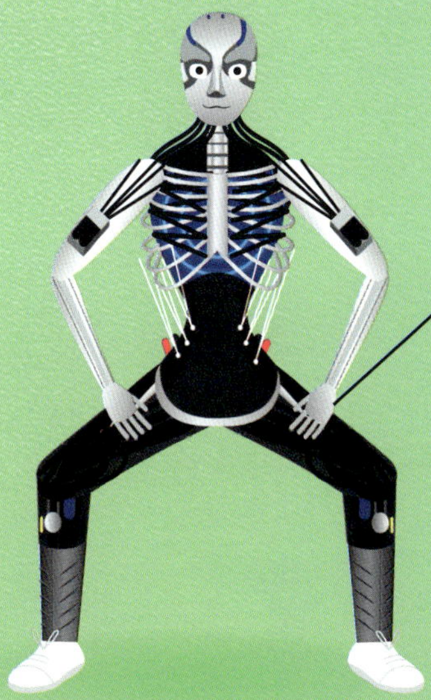

Five-digit hands and feet

The robot's parts are moved by 108 electric motors.

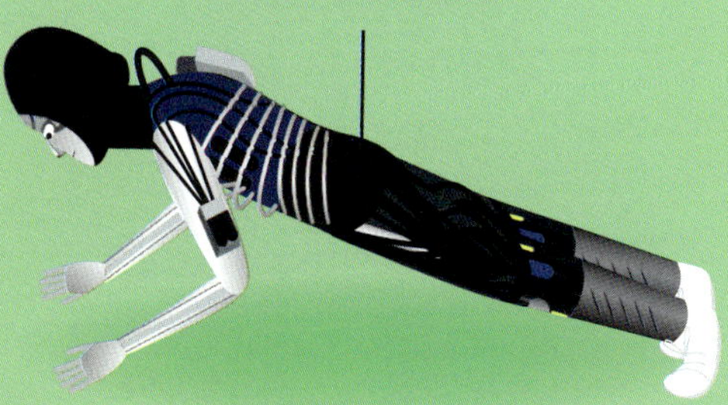

GAMES ROBOTS PLAY

Playing games may be fun, but for robots, computers, and the researchers who work with them, it's a serious business. Many projects use strategy games to test a robot or computer's ability to learn, predict, and react to events in order to make smarter decisions. This often involves analyzing vast amounts of data.

98% ...

... the percentage of games Baxter, once trained, won against human opponents.

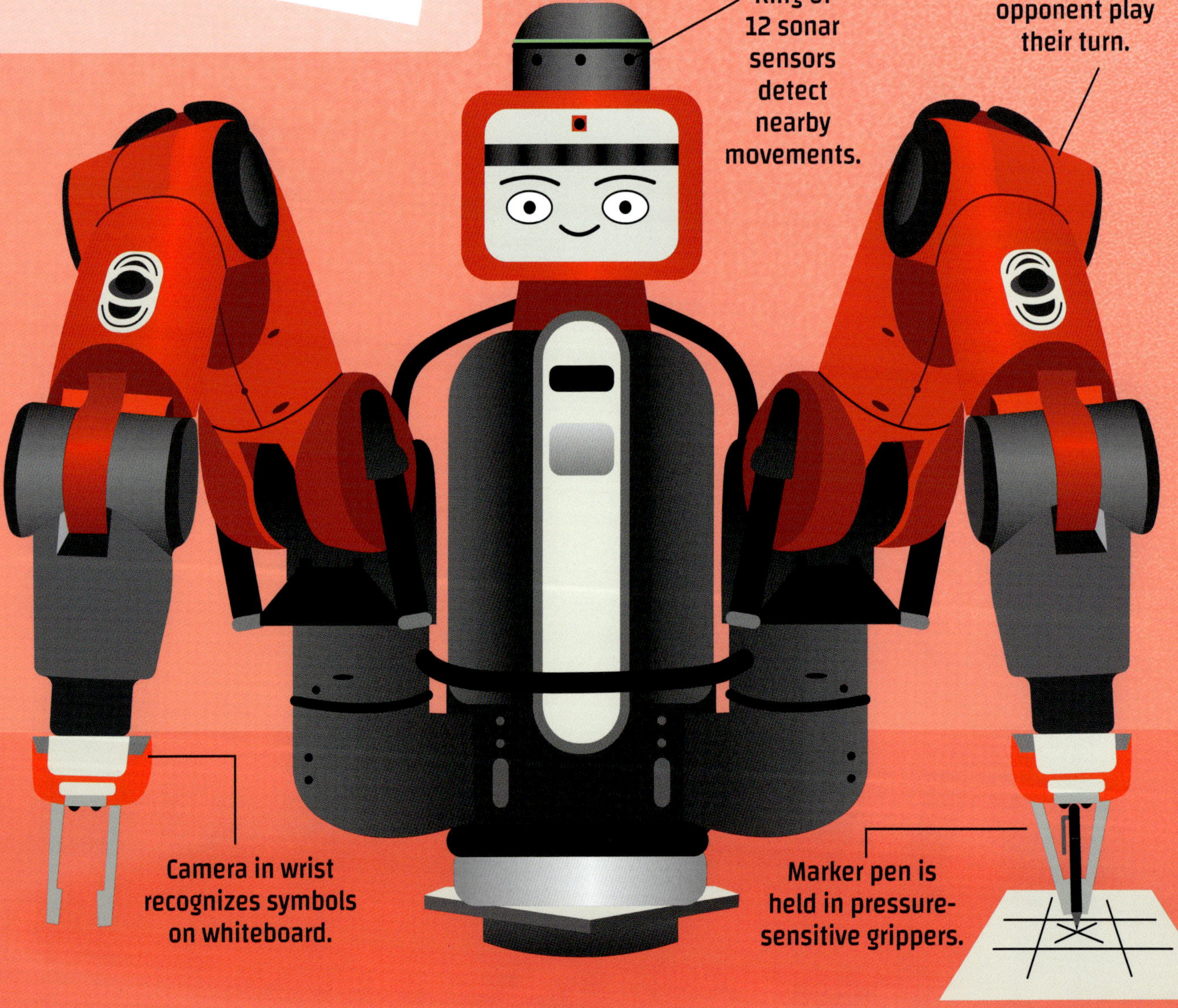

MACHINE LEARNING

A robot or computer that can learn the rules and tactics of games could be capable of learning many other things. That's why researchers equipped a Baxter robot (left) with a pen to play tic-tac-toe. The robot trained itself in the best ways to play this and other games, such as Connect 4 (left), by trial and error.

ROBOCUP

There's a lot of thinking as well as action in the RoboCup robotic football competition. The 2019 tournament, held in Australia, attracted 170 teams. Many took part in the 4-robot-a-side standard competition using Nao humanoid robots.

30 ...

... the number of decisions a RoboCup robot may need to make each second to track the ball, opponents, and teammates and decide on its next move.

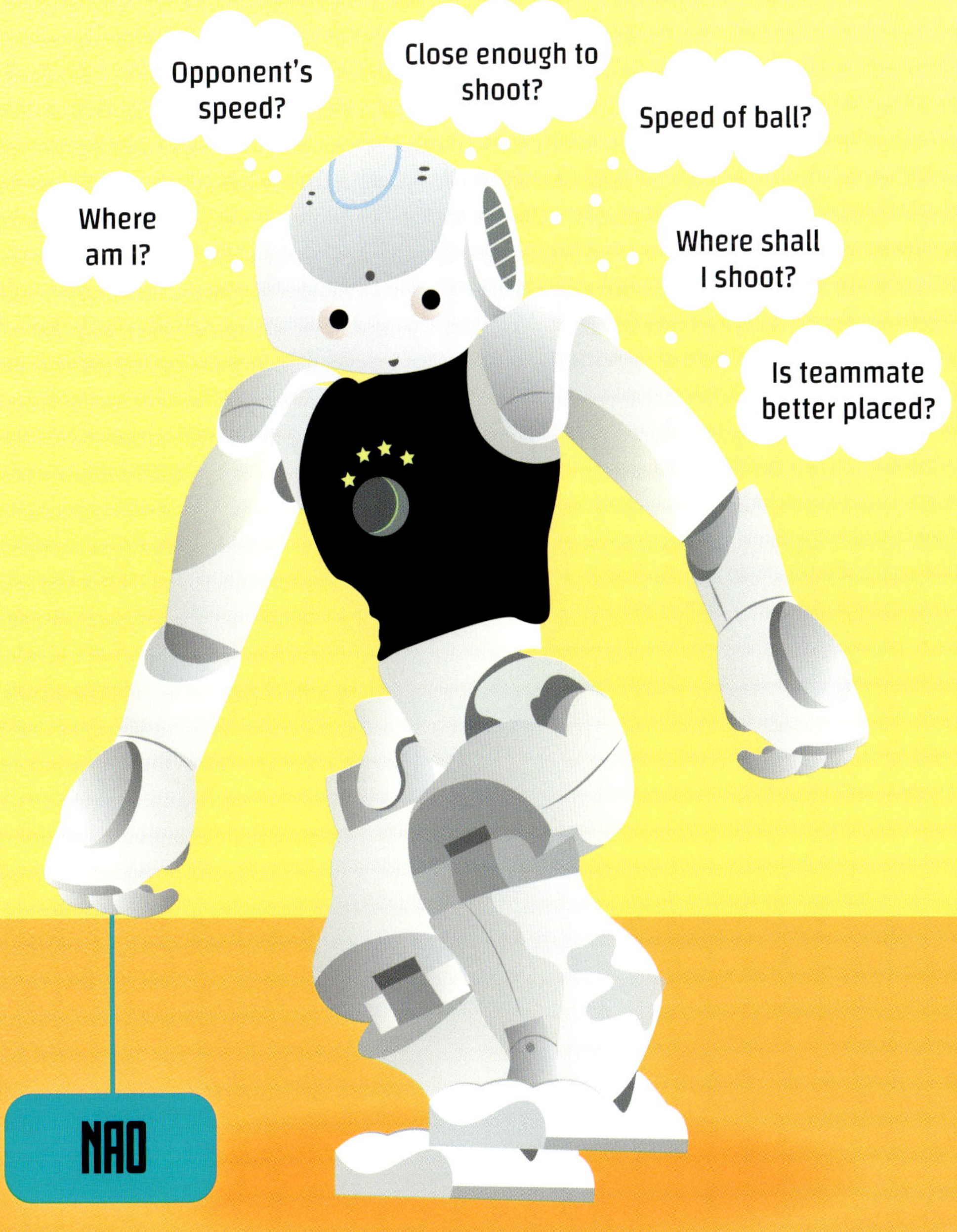

BACK TO SCHOOL

Robots can be taught by uploading programs, containing thousands of lines of code, into their memory. It's also possible to teach a robot while it is running to perform the actions needed to complete a task. Just as robots can learn from people, so people can learn from building, programming, and working with robots.

TEACH PENDANTS

These tablet devices allow a user to instruct a robot by moving it from point to point and performing actions all in a sequence. Each stage of the task is recorded and stored in memory so that the whole task can be repeated by the robot on its own again and again.

ROBOTS TEACHING ROBOTS

Researchers at the Massachusetts Institute of Technology have created a knowledge base of how different objects can be handled by machines. When a human demonstrates a task, the robot accesses the knowledge base so it can perform the task itself. The robot can then teach the same task to another robot, even one of a completely different shape and size.

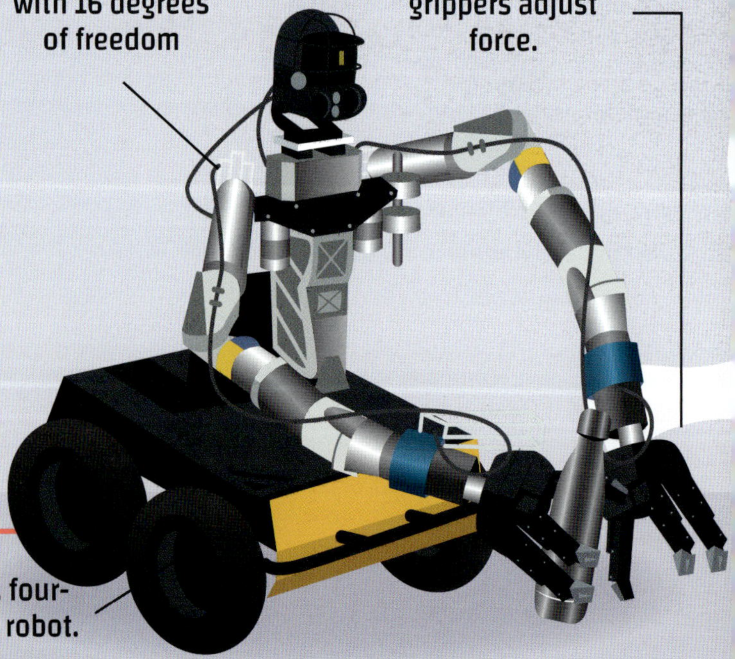

Having learned how to pick up a metal flask containing chemicals, Optimus (below left) is now teaching Atlas how to do the same.

The robots communicate via radio signals.

... the success rate of Optimus teaching Atlas tasks by itself in trials.

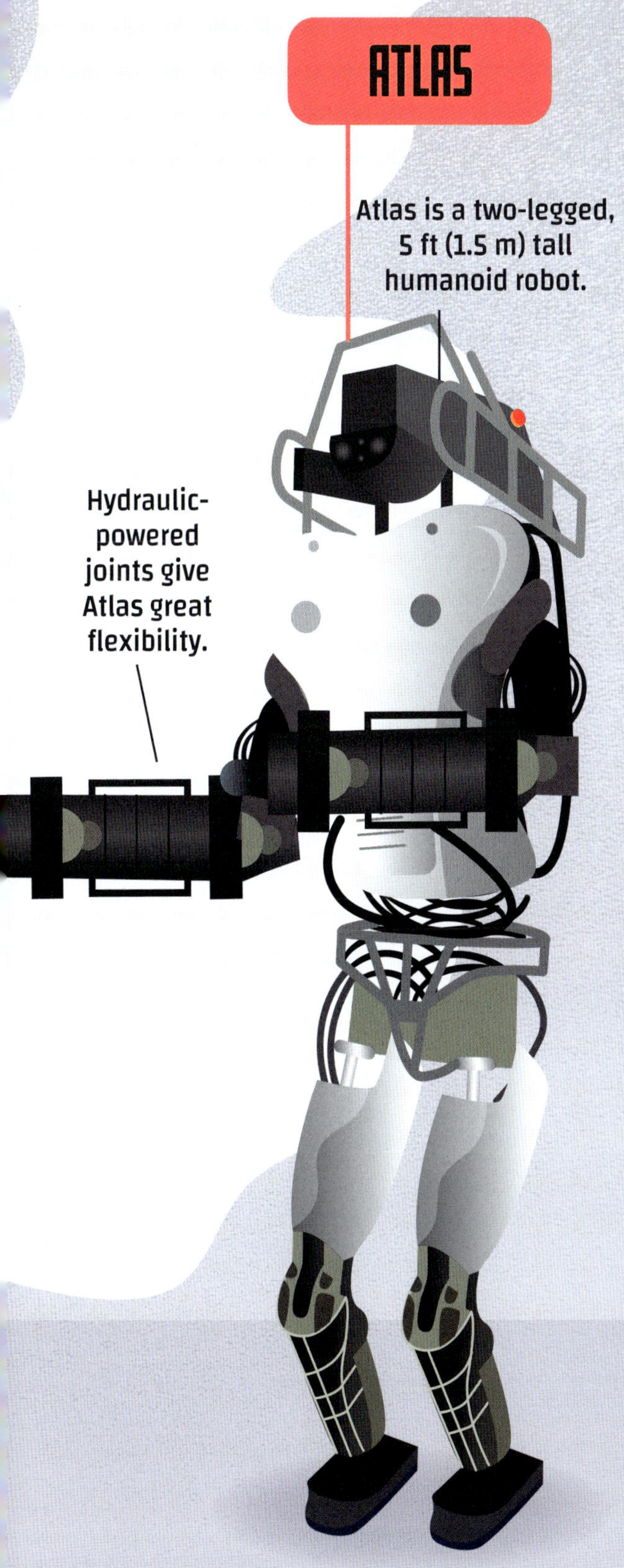

ROBOTS TEACHING PEOPLE

There's no better way to learn about robots than to build, program, and operate one. Hundreds of different humanoid, wheeled, and static educational robots allow users to modify bots and code new tasks.

Lego Mindstorms®

Krypton 3

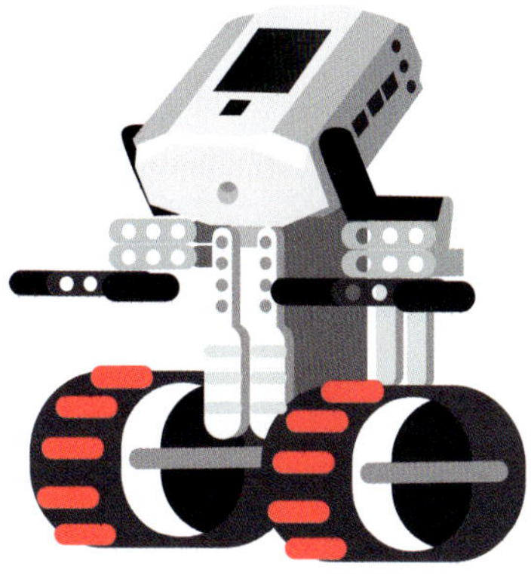

Marty

MACHINE LEARNING

For a machine to be artificially intelligent, it needs to be capable of planning, reasoning, and solving problems. Machine learning is getting robots to learn by themselves from information they gather rather than people controlling them. Some robots can build their own knowledge bases or use trial and error to work out the best way to perform a task.

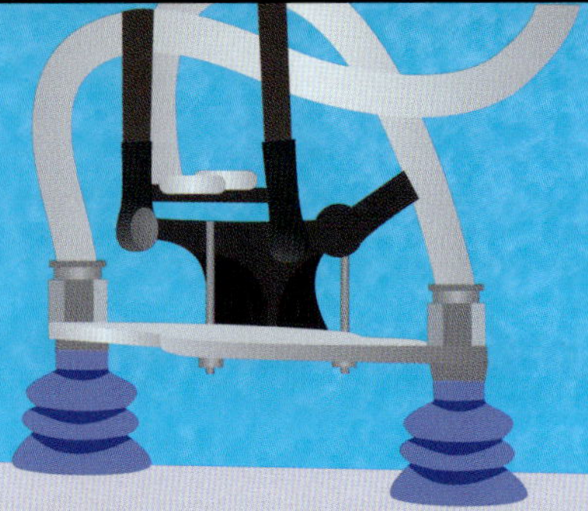

Clarke, a garbage-picking robot in Denver, CO, uses its controller and camera to learn what shape and color recyclable objects are so it can gather them at a faster rate.

60 OBJECTS PER MINUTE

50% FASTER THAN HUMANS

Top speed: 3 ft (1 m) per second

Robot can climb 14-in (35 cm) high steps and 20-degree slopes.

Controller plots path avoiding obstacles and calculates quickest route.

LiDAR sensor sweeps the surroundings as robot builds up map of its environment.

ANYMAL C

ANYMAL C

This four-legged robot handles masses of data sent back every second by its LiDAR and other sensors to map the space it is moving in. The robot can continually adjust its shape and leg position to suit the terrain, while plotting the best route to its target.

Weight: 110 lb (50 kg)

Dimensions: 41 in x 20 in x 33 in (105 cm × 52 cm × 83 cm)

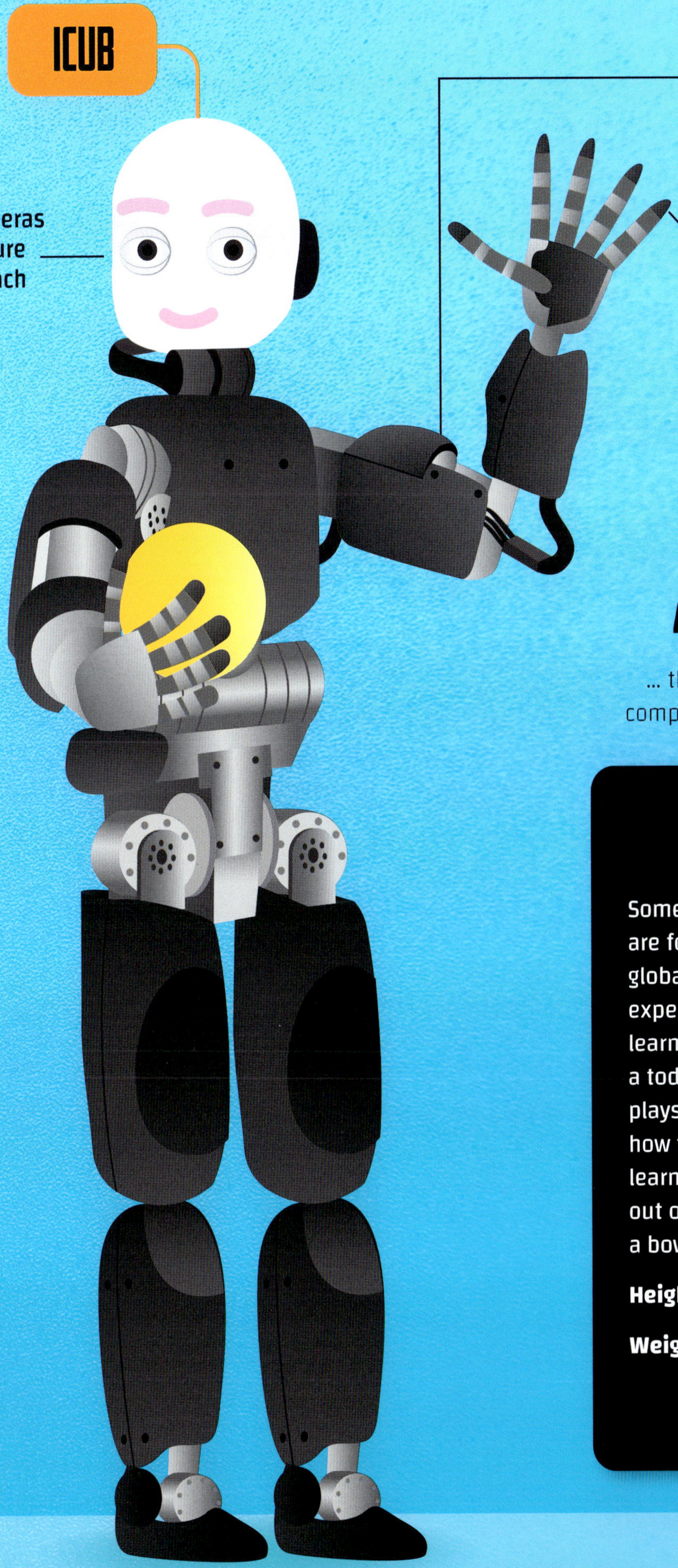

4,000,000 ...

... the number of lines of computer code running iCub.

ICUB

Some 40 Italian iCub robots are found in robotics labs globally where researchers are experimenting with ways robots can learn for themselves. Looking like a toddler and just as curious, iCub plays with objects to understand how to use them. iCubs have learned to crawl, create structures out of building blocks, and even fire a bow and arrow.

Height: 41 in (104 cm)

Weight: 51-55 lb (23-25 kg)

ALMOST HUMAN?

Some humanoid robots have been built to look and act just like humans, even if they don't possess people's versatility and intelligence. These robots are used in media and public relations or to further research into artificial intelligence and how to make robots learn and act more like us.

The UK's Ai-Da robot (left) scans a scene via cameras in her eyes. Data from the images are run through a set of programming rules, called an algorithm, to create a jagged, abstract outline which is drawn onto the page by the robot. A human artist fills in the color.

$1,250,000+...

... the money made so far from sales of Ai-Da's drawings and paintings.

SUPER SOPHIA

Few robots have given TED talks, appeared on TV chat shows, or interviewed world leaders. But then, few robots are quite like Sophia. This Hong Kong humanoid robot uses AI to recognize and react to people's emotions from their facial expression and tone of voice. Sophia also uses natural language processing to try to understand questions and give a meaningful reply.

Gripping hands can hold range of tools including pencil with which she can sketch.

Lightweight aluminium arms contain many 3D-printed parts.

60 ...

...the number of facial expressions Sophia can make via **33** servos (electric motors) pulling cords attached to the inside of the facial skin.

In 2017, Sophia was both made a citizen of Saudi Arabia and the first non-human United Nations ambassador! She visited **38** countries in 2019.

16 ...

... the number of motors that move the face parts of humanoid robot, Jiang Lailai. This robot became a co-host of a science news TV show in China in 2019.

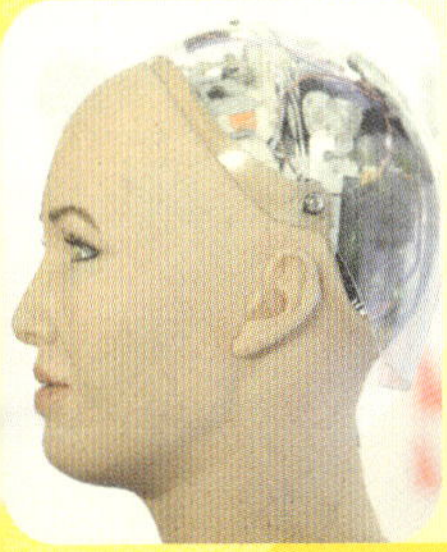

A transparent dome covers the robot's controller electronics.

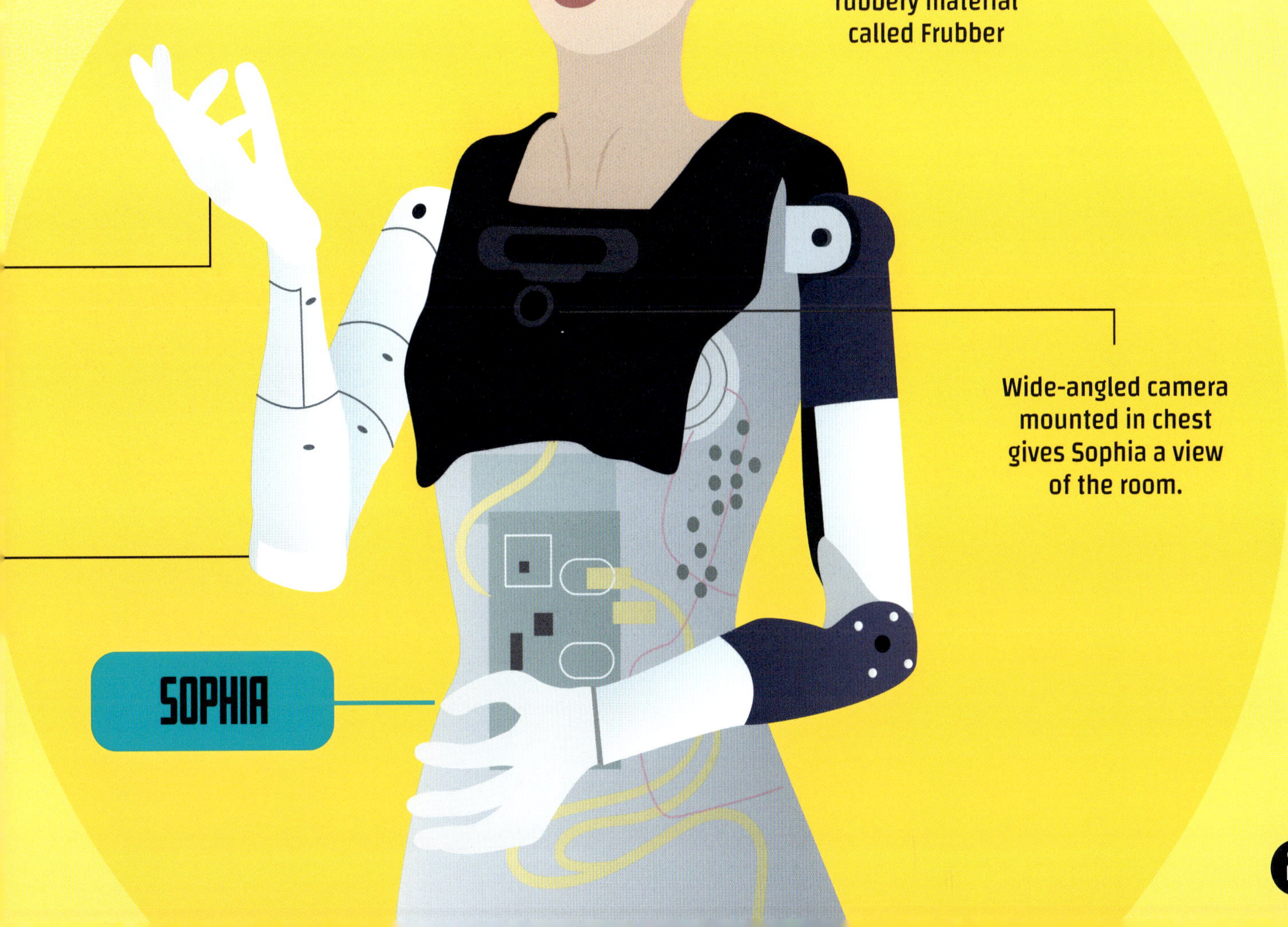

A SMART FUTURE?

No one knows quite how smart robots will become in the future, but it's certain there will be advances in how they sense, make decisions, and operate. Robots and other machines are likely to become much more common and more involved in people's lives.

300,000,000 ...

... the number of driverless vehicles predicted to be on the world's roads in 2050.

TECHNICAL ADVANCES

Advances in technology could help make robots more intelligent and useful. Better batteries could allow mobile and social robots to operate for longer periods between recharges. New, smart materials, may lead to robots which can change shape to perform different tasks.

KNOW-IT-ALLS

Faster connectivity may lead to robots being able to access almost unlimited stores of data about you. Future personal robots may be able to offer all kinds of help, at work and play.

More intelligent sensors and controllers could enable robots to work with each other closely in '"lights-out" factories – free of humans so there's no need for lighting or heating.

50 ...

... the estimated number of big robots built each day by robots in FANUC's lights-out factory in Japan. Human staff only visit once every 600 working hours to check if maintenance is needed.

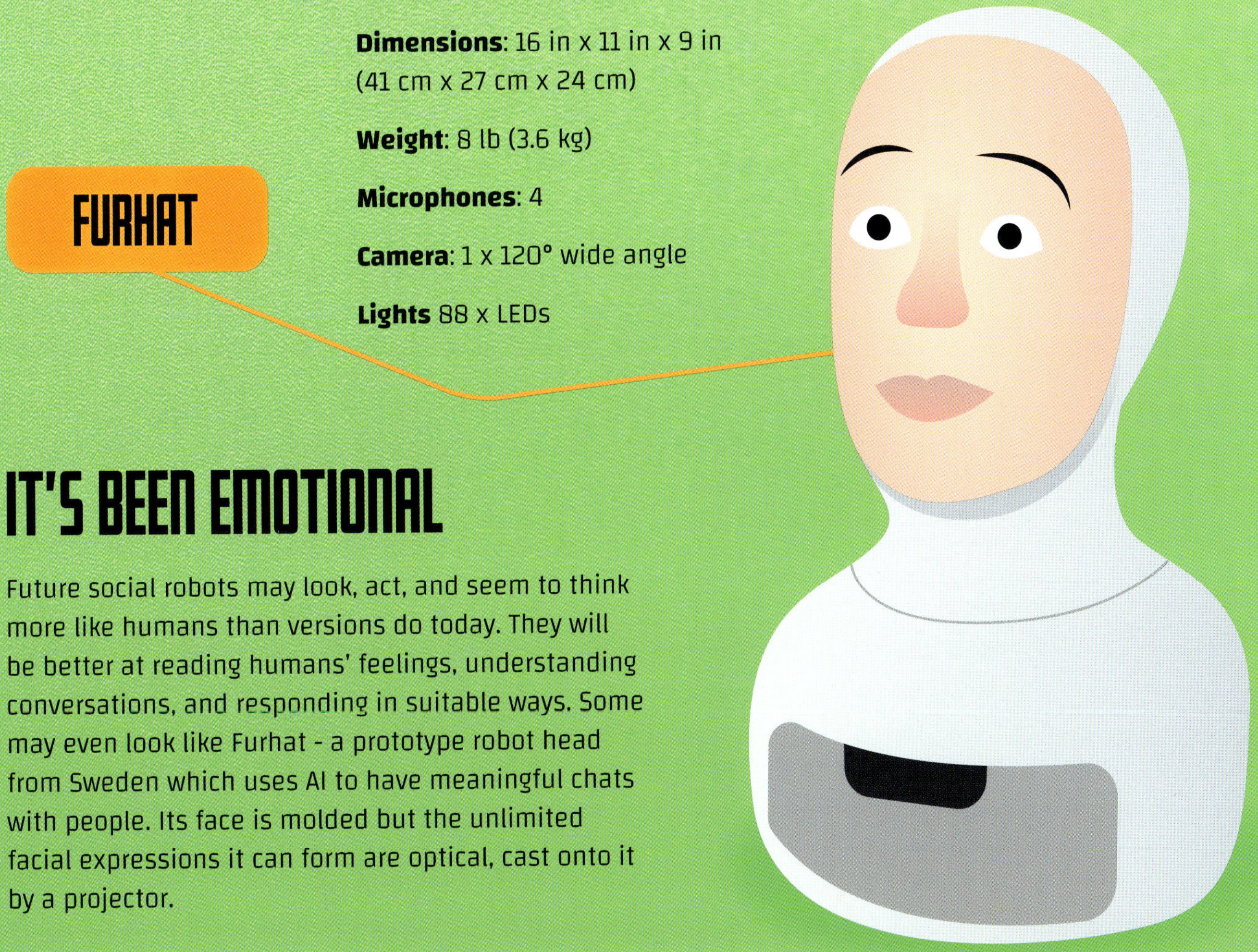

IT'S BEEN EMOTIONAL

Future social robots may look, act, and seem to think more like humans than versions do today. They will be better at reading humans' feelings, understanding conversations, and responding in suitable ways. Some may even look like Furhat - a prototype robot head from Sweden which uses AI to have meaningful chats with people. Its face is molded but the unlimited facial expressions it can form are optical, cast onto it by a projector.

QUIZ

Try this quiz to find out how much you can remember about super smart robots. The answers are at the bottom of the page.

1. In which country was the 2019 RoboCup tournament held?

a) Australia

b) Japan

c) Slovakia

2. How many legs does the ANYmal C have?

a) Two

b) Four

c) Six

3. What is the name of the humanoid robot made a UN ambassador in 2017?

a) Sophia

b) Jian Lailai

c) Baxter

4. How long is the Cimon-2 robot's mission in space planned to last?

a) Six months

b) One year

c) Three years

5. How many sensors will you find in a NAO robot?

a) More than 20

b) More than 35

c) More than 50

6. Who was the human world chess champion that the IBM Deep Blue computer beat in 1997?

a) Magnus Carlsen

b) Garry Kasparov

c) Bobby Fischer

7. How many lines of computer code are used to run the robot iCub?

a) 500,000

b) 1,500,000

c) 4,000,000

8. How many cameras are used in a Waymo driverless car?

a) 12

b) 29

c) 67

9. Which robot, built by Cynthia Breazeal, had 15 degrees of freedom and could express nine emotions?

a) Kismet

b) Ai-Da

c) Leka

10. How far did the Stanley driverless car navigate by itself in 2005?

a) 22 miles (36 km)

b) 88 miles (142 km)

c) 175 miles (281 km)

Answers

1 a, 2 b, 3.a, 4.c, 5.c, 6.b, 7.c, 8.b, 9.a, 10.c

GLOSSARY

autonomous
Describes a machine that can make decisions and works by itself.

cloud computing
The storage of data and use of apps and programs on computers accessed over the Internet.

computer network
Two or more computers linked together so they can exchange messages and data.

controller
The part of the robot which makes decisions and tells the other parts of the robot what to do. It is usually a computer.

database
An organized collection of information that allows data to be easily searched and retrieved.

degrees of freedom
The different ways and directions in which a robot or its parts can move.

evaporate
To turn from a liquid into a gas.

feedback
Useful information about a situation or how a task is going, sent back to the robot by its sensors.

Global Positioning System (GPS)
A navigation system using a series of satellites orbiting Earth to give an accurate position on Earth.

humanoid
Describes a robot that has a partial or complete human-like appearance or one that performs human-like actions.

infrared
A type of electromagnetic radiation, like light, but not visible to our eyes.

LiDAR
Short for Light Detection And Ranging, this is a sensor system that sends out pulses of laser light to measure distances to objects.

prototype
A first version of a device made to test it out or to raise publicity.

sensor
A device that collects information about a robot or its surroundings.

supercomputer
A particularly powerful, high-performance computer used for exceptionally complex tasks.

ultrasonic
Describes sound waves that exist above the range of human hearing.

FURTHER INFORMATION

Books

A Robot World – Clive Gifford, Cavendish Square, 2024

Explore AI: Intelligent Robots – Sonya Newland, Wayland, 2021

The Tech-Head Guide: AI – William Potter, Wayland, 2021

Websites

https://www.youtube.com/watch?v=kB5Bg2277Pg&index=70&list=PLslScfOUDB71T4yQqtCXCdviViNigDBap
See ASIMO and two other advanced humanoid robots in action.

https://www.youtube.com/watch?v=KTpRiPFbmuE
See how iCub learns about objects and compares it to others with this BBC video.

https://www.youtube.com/watch?v=5_jp9CwJhcA
Watch the social robot Sophia answer questions in an interview.

INDEX